APR 0 3 2018

INTRO TO
EVENTING

BY WHITNEY SANDERSON

SADDLE UP!

SportsZone

An Imprint of Abdo Publishing
abdopublishing.com

abdopublishing.com

Published by Abdo Publishing, a division of ABDO, PO Box 398166, Minneapolis, Minnesota 55439. Copyright © 2018 by Abdo Consulting Group, Inc. International copyrights reserved in all countries. No part of this book may be reproduced in any form without written permission from the publisher. SportsZone™ is a trademark and logo of Abdo Publishing.

Printed in the United States of America, North Mankato, Minnesota
092017
012018

Cover Photo: iStockphoto
Interior Photos: iStockphoto, 1, 15, 26, 33, 39, 44; Scott Barbour/AUS/Allsport/Getty Images Sport/Getty Images, 5; Scott Barbour/Allsport/Getty Images Sport/Getty Images, 7; Sergio Perez/Reuters/Newscom, 9; Topical Press Agency/Hulton Archive/Getty Images, 10–11; John Locher/AP Images, 13; NurPhoto/Getty Images, 17; Eric Ferguson/iStockphoto, 18; Bjorn Larsson Rosvall/TT News Agency/AP Images, 20; John Rich/iStockphoto, 23; Shutterstock Images, 25; Andrew Matthews/PA Wire URN:31201203/AP Images, 28–29; Chung/LNP/Rex Features/AP Images, 31; Pascal Le Segretain/Getty Images Entertainment/Getty Images, 35; Davide Mombelli/Corbis Sport/Getty Images, 36–37; Stephen McCarthy/Sportsfile/Getty Images, 40; Candice Chavez/Eclipse Sportswire/Getty Images Sport/Getty Images, 42–43

Editor: Marie Pearson
Series Designer: Laura Polzin
Content Consultant: Paige Clark, B.S. equine science, University of Minnesota Crookston

Publisher's Cataloging-in-Publication Data
Names: Sanderson, Whitney, author.
Title: Intro to eventing / by Whitney Sanderson.
Description: Minneapolis, Minnesota : Abdo Publishing, 2018. | Series: Saddle up! | Includes online resources and index.
Identifiers: LCCN 2017946874 | ISBN 9781532113406 (lib.bdg.) | ISBN 9781532152283 (ebook)
Subjects: LCSH: Eventing (Horsemanship)--Juvenile literature. | Horsemanship--Juvenile literature. | Horse sports--Juvenile literature.
Classification: DDC 798.24--dc23
LC record available at https://lccn.loc.gov/2017946874

TABLE OF
CONTENTS

THE EQUINE TRIATHLON

I't's a sunny September afternoon at the 2000 Olympic Games in Sydney, Australia. A large sand arena is set up with a course of colorful jumps. United States team member David O'Connor rides through the arena gate on an elegant dark bay gelding named Custom Made. A gelding is a male horse surgically made unable to reproduce. The 17.2-hand Irish sport horse is called Tailor for short.

Tailor is a triathlete of the horse world. He competes in dressage, cross-country, and show jumping. He has

David O'Connor and Tailor head for a jump in the 2000 Olympic Games.

been trained for many years to reach this level. His diet and exercise are as carefully planned as any human Olympian's.

Today is the final day of individual eventing. It has been 16 years since the United States has taken home an Olympic gold in eventing. O'Connor and Tailor have already ridden a nearly perfect dressage test and have had a clean round in cross-country. Now Tailor's ears prick forward as he looks over the jumps.

O'Connor is nervous. Show jumping is Tailor's weakness. Sometimes the horse does not lift his hooves carefully and knocks rails down. Each time that happens, five penalty points are added to the pair's score. In eventing, the lowest score wins. If O'Connor and Tailor drop rails at more than two of the 15 jumps, the gold medal may slip from their grasp.

O'Connor urges Tailor into a canter, and they head toward the first fence. Tailor clears it easily. But the gelding is tired. Yesterday, he jumped more than 30 cross-country fences, galloping for 13 minutes straight.

O'Connor and Tailor leap over a jump.

Today he's surrounded by distracting sights, sounds, and smells. But Tailor trusts David and stays focused.

They jump the next five fences cleanly. Then the gelding's hooves hit the top of a green gate. O'Connor listens for the *thud* of a falling rail. It wobbles but stays up. When he turns his attention back to the course, he's forgotten where the next jump is. He slows Tailor down and looks wildly around. If he misses the fence or jumps the wrong one, they'll be eliminated.

People in the crowd are shouting, trying to guide him. Then O'Connor remembers the wall. He aims Tailor at the solid brick fence, and they're back on track. At the ninth fence, Tailor knocks down a rail. His strides get uneven for a moment, but O'Connor steadies him. They head into a tough triple combination, and Tailor clears each jump. They gallop between the finish flags less than a second before the clock runs out. Despite their near disaster on the course, they have won the gold in eventing with just 34 penalty points—the lowest score in Olympic history!

WHAT IS EVENTING?

Back when horses were used in war, cavalry units needed fit, well-trained mounts that were brave enough to tackle any obstacle. Eventing began as a way for officers to

O'Connor and Tailor lead a victory lap, celebrating their Olympic gold medal in eventing.

Eventing began as a way to test a warhorse's ability to perform important tasks such as carrying a rider down a steep hill.

test their horses. The first official event took place at the Olympic Games in 1912. It was called "The Militaire," and it was open only to officers in an army. But by the middle of the 1900s, large firearms eliminated the need for warhorses. More people began riding for sport.

The United States Eventing Association (USEA) was
formed in 1959. It creates the rules for events in the United
States. At events where people from different countries
ride together, the Fédération Équestre Internationale (FEI)
sets the guidelines. Eventing competitions—sometimes

called horse trials or combined training—often take place over three days. The first day is dressage, the second is cross-country jumping, and the third is show jumping. At lower-level events, all three phases might take place on the same day. The USEA has seven levels of eventing, from beginner-novice to advanced. The FEI has seven levels too. The FEI entry level is CIC* (one star), and the highest is CCI**** (four star). Dressage and show jumping are also individual competitions.

Each phase of eventing requires a different set of skills. Like O'Connor and Tailor, most competitors have a strongest and a weakest event. Even Olympic riders can find areas to improve their skills and their relationship with their horses. This makes the sport challenging and fun.

FAMOUS NAMES

Some of the most well-known top-level FEI events are the Rolex Kentucky Three-Day Event, the Australian International Three-Day Event, and the Burghley and Badminton Horse Trials in England. Many top riders, including Michael Jung, Karen O'Connor, and Phillip Dutton, travel across the world with their horses to compete in these events.

Cross-country jumps test a horse's trust in its rider.

2

DRESSAGE: BALANCE AND PARTNERSHIP

Dressage comes from a French word that means "to train." The dressage phase in eventing shows harmony between horse and rider. The horse should listen to the rider, and the rider should give the horse quiet, correct cues. The test is ridden in a flat, fenced-in arena. Each horse and rider follows a set pattern of movements, called a test, at the walk, trot, and canter.

In dressage, the horse should bend gracefully into turns.

In dressage, the horse should bend gracefully. The horse should place more weight on its hind legs so that its steps look light but powerful and balanced. Dressage is judged on performance. A well-ridden test is beautiful to watch. It can look as if the horse and rider are dancing.

CHECKING GEAR

Only certain types of bits are allowed in dressage. A steward must check each horse's bit, as well as any whips or spurs, before the test. The steward checks the horse for any marks or injuries that might indicate the rider trains with too much force. This ensures that the horse performs because of good training, not fear of punishment.

PREPARATIONS

Competitors dress up for dressage day. Horses' manes are braided, ears and whiskers are clipped, and hooves are coated in polish. Many riders use a special dressage saddle, which has a deeper seat and a longer flap than a jumping saddle. This helps riders feel the horse move and send signals through their legs. The saddle is worn with a square white pad. A girth under the horse's belly holds them in place. At lower levels, some people use one all-purpose saddle and bridle.

The movements in dressage are both elegant and powerful.

The rider's outfit for dressage is white or tan breeches, knee-high black leather boots and gloves. The coat is black with four buttons. It is worn over a white show shirt with a tie or pin at the collar. Riders wear a safety helmet or top hat. They also wear entry numbers on their jackets and on their horses' bridles.

RIDING THE TEST

A bell signals the beginning of each rider's test, and the horse and rider have 45 seconds to enter the arena. Dressage arenas are marked with letters along the outside of the arena, with an X in the center. Every movement in a dressage test starts and ends at a letter. For example, a test might say "trot BE." This means the rider must trot the horse from sign B to sign E.

Lower-level dressage tests ask for simple changes of gait and direction, as well as shapes such as circles. At higher levels, horses are asked to collect (shorten) or extend (lengthen) their strides. They must also be able to move sideways, or laterally. Movements get more difficult as a horse and rider advance in their training.

Every test ends with the rider halting at X. The rider puts both reins in one hand, drops his or her right arm down straight, and nods to the judge as a sign of respect. The pair can then walk out of the arena on a loose rein.

Signs with letters surround the dressage arena.

WHAT'S THE SCORE?

Each movement in dressage is worth 10 points. A score of zero means the horse and rider didn't complete the movement at all. A 10 means it was done perfectly. Judges look at several factors to decide each score. They look for whether the horse moves willingly without seeming lazy or rushed. They look for qualities such as correctness and harmony in the movements. Any movements that the horse and rider did not perform perfectly give them penalty points. These are carried over to the next phase.

For many horses, dressage is the hardest part of eventing because of the balance it requires. But smart event riders spend a lot of time on dressage. If a horse can easily adjust its stride, bend, and shift its weight back to its hind legs, it will be a stronger competitor.

Glock's Flirt, ridden by Hans Peter Minderhoud, moves laterally across the arena.

CROSS-COUNTRY: SPEED AND STAMINA

Cross-country tests a horse's stamina in jumping and galloping for long distances. It also tests a rider's knowledge of jumping and the horse's bravery and fitness. Courses are several miles long, winding through a mix of open fields and woods. Most jumps are made from natural materials such as logs, wooden planks, brush, and hay bales. Riders walk the course ahead of time and plan how

Cross-country jumps are solid and won't fall over if the horse hits them.

they will approach each fence. A beginner-novice course has 14 to 18 jumps that are up to 31 inches (79 cm) high. Advanced courses have 30 to 45 jumps up to 47 inches (120 cm) high. Most cross-country fences are wide and sturdy, making them look even bigger.

THE GEAR

For cross-country, riders wear breeches, field boots, a comfortable shirt, and gloves with a good grip. Riders must wear a safety vest for cross-country. A helmet and a medical armband are also required. A medical armband is a form with the rider's medical history, worn in case of an injury during cross-country or show jumping.

Horses wear an all-purpose or jumping saddle. A breastplate prevents the saddle from slipping back. Cross-country tack, or gear, might also include a

SAFETY

Safety is a top concern in eventing. In cross-country, riders may put grease on their horses' legs to help them slide over a fence if they have trouble clearing it. Horses might also wear studs, or small pieces of metal, on their shoes to help grip wet or slippery ground.

Cross-country is a dangerous sport, so helmets, safety vests, and medical armbands are important for keeping the rider safe and making sure he or she can receive quick care in an emergency.

martingale, a leather strap that keeps the horse from tossing up its head. Splint boots and bell boots protect the horse's legs and hooves. Their manes and tails are left natural.

RIDING THE COURSE

At the beginning of the course, each horse and rider must wait in a three-sided start box. After the signal, they're off! The first few jumps on a cross-country course are easy. Each jump is marked with flags on each corner. The rider must keep the white flag on the left and red on the right. A fence judge stands to the side of each jump and marks if there were any penalty points at that obstacle.

The fences get more difficult as the course goes on. Types of jumps include brush fences, hay bales, and holes in the ground called ditches. There are also banks where the horse leaps up onto a grassy surface and then down the other side. The horse usually must jump into water at least once. Some jumps have options where the rider can choose a more difficult route to save time or an easier route to save the horse's stamina.

Horses may have to run through the water and then leap onto a platform.

27

Jumps can get both taller and wider at higher levels.

PENALTY POINTS

If a horse and rider jump all the cross-country fences
within the time allowed, they will receive zero penalty

points. But things don't always go smoothly. They get penalty points if a horse stops in front of a fence or refuses a jump. Three refusals eliminate the pair from the competition. Each course has an optimal time in which to complete it. Every second over that time is more penalty points. If the horse and rider take longer than twice the optimal time to complete the course or if they fall, they're eliminated. However, at the beginner-novice and novice levels, if the rider manages to land on his or her feet, he or she will get 45 penalty points instead.

STRATEGIES FOR SUCCESS

Cross-country courses are ridden at faster speeds as the level goes up. A steady canter is just right to finish a beginner-novice course. By the advanced level, the horse must keep up a fast gallop, slowing down only a little for the fences. Horses need a lot of conditioning to be fit for this phase.

Because of the fast speed and solid jumps, falls and injuries happen most often in cross-country. Practicing as many types of jumps as possible and riding up and down hills and over different types of ground gives the horse confidence and good balance, reducing falls. Riders should walk the course carefully, planning how to ride difficult jumps. Riders should also compete at a lower

A horse has to be in top shape to maintain speed throughout a cross-country course.

level than they practice at home. This way the horse will be fit and won't be frightened by big jumps.

AFTER THE COURSE

When the hard work of a cross-country course is finished, horses must be walked until they are cool and their heart rate has returned to normal, 28 to 40 beats per minute. Riders should check hooves and legs for injury. The horse is often given a cool bath with a hose or sponge to remove dirt and sweat. If the horse has sweated a lot, the rider or groom might give it extra salt and electrolytes.

Horses must pass a vet check after the cross-country phase before they go on to show jumping. The rider leads the horse while the veterinarian watches it trot for a short distance to make sure that it is not injured and is able to continue.

The cross-country course pushes the horse and rider's stamina to the limit. But many riders say that the joy of galloping and jumping across beautiful countryside is their favorite part of the sport.

CROSS-COUNTRY GEAR

SAFETY VEST

HELMET

BREECHES

MEDICAL ARMBAND

GLOVES

JUMPING SADDLE

FIELD BOOTS

BREASTPLATE

MARTINGALE

SPLINT BOOTS

BELL BOOTS

4

SHOW JUMPING: POWER AND PRECISION

The last phase of eventing tests whether or not the horse is still fit and willing after the first two trials. Like in cross-country, riders walk the show jumping course before they ride. They look for areas where they will need to steady and balance the horse, speed up, or jump at an angle.

A rider studies a path over the jumps in preparation for her ride.

Giulia Martinengo Marquet and Fixdesign Funke clear an oxer at the 2015 Piazza di Siena in Rome.

Show jumps are a few inches taller than cross-country fences at most levels. Advanced show jumps may be up to 49 inches (124 cm) high. Each type of fence offers a different challenge. Vertical fences ask a horse to jump

high and carefully. Horses must make a wide leap over
oxer jumps, which have two or three rails the horse has
to clear all at once. In a combination, the horse needs to
keep its rhythm and balance over two or three closely

spaced fences. There is usually a water jump, where the horse must leap across a rectangular pool. If the horse's hooves touch the water, the pair gets four faults. Even simple show jumps may have wild colors or decorations that test a horse's willingness to jump.

TACK AND ATTIRE

The rider's outfit for show jumping is similar to that for dressage. A rider wears buff or tan breeches, field boots, and a black, navy blue, hunter green, or gray coats. Very high-level riders may wear red (called "pink") coats. The rider may carry a short crop or wear spurs to encourage the horse if it hesitates.

Jumping tack is often in shades of brown. Jumping saddles tend to have a shorter flap and a shallower seat than dressage saddles. This allows the rider to rise up out of the saddle over a jump. A belly guard attached to the girth helps keep the horse from hitting its underside with its own hooves when jumping over a fence. The horse's boots for show jumping often have an open front, which

Riders should keep their eyes forward when jumping.

keeps the horse's legs protected but lets it feel the touch of a rail. This encourages the horse to be careful.

THE LAST SCORE

Show jumping courses are shorter than cross-country, but they require speed and accuracy. There are 12 to 15 fences, and the time allowed is just a few minutes. But they are important minutes. Even if a horse and rider have had two clean phases, they could still fall out of the ribbons if they make a mistake.

Show jump rails are set in shallow cups. A light brush from a horse's hooves can bring them crashing down. Some horses are less careful with their legs, but others take care to tuck up their legs. Valuable event horses are those with the ability to clear big jumps with ease. Pairs get penalty points if a horse knocks a rail or refuses a fence, if the rider falls, or if they are over the time limit. If a horse falls or has three refusals, the team is eliminated.

The penalty points from all three phases are added together. The team with the lowest score wins. Top scores

Horses must keep their back hooves tucked to avoid knocking rails.

in the 20s are common when riders have only faults from dressage. But some cross-country and show jumping courses are so hard that no one has a clear round. In this case a rider might win with 40 or more penalties.

Ribbons are awarded for the top six or 10 places, with a trophy, plaque, or Olympic medal for the winner. Sometimes there are prizes such as grooming supplies, tack, or gift certificates. Some high-level events have prize money. At Kentucky Rolex, $400,000 is divided among the top 20 finishers.

WHO EVENTS?

A horse doesn't need to be expensive or purebred to be a good

Michael Jung won the Kentucky Rolex in 2015, 2016, and 2017.

Riders of all ages on horses or ponies can compete in eventing.

eventer. Hard work and courage are more important. Solid training is the key to success. Lower-level events are filled with many horses and ponies, from tiny Shetland ponies to huge Clydesdales. At the highest levels, Thoroughbreds and warmbloods are most often seen. These breeds tend to be natural athletes. Horses bred and trained for eventing are called sport horses.

Most people must take lessons for a few years before they have the balance and control needed for eventing. The USEA says riders must be at least 14 years old to compete at the preliminary level, 16 for intermediate, and 18 for advanced. The USEA has a Young Riders program to help eventers under 21 gain show experience. Many riders, whether they show at the beginner-novice level for fun or travel across the world to compete, say there is no other horse sport that compares to the challenge and thrill of eventing.

YOUNG RIDER SPOTLIGHT

Delaney Vaden started eventing at age 10 on a pony that didn't much like to jump. But Delaney stuck with it. Her new horse, RedRox Jazzman—a Clydesdale, Thoroughbred, and quarter horse cross—loves cross-country. In 2016, when Delaney was 14, she and Jazz took home the $15,000 Preliminary Challenge prize at the Woodside event in California. Delaney plans to move up to even higher levels when she is old enough.

GLOSSARY

CANTER

A horse's three-beat gait that is faster than a trot but slower than a gallop.

CONDITIONING

Riding to make a horse fit for competition.

CROP

A short riding whip.

GAIT

The way a horse moves its feet in order to travel forward.

GALLOP

A fast four-beat run.

GIRTH

A strap that runs from one side of the saddle, under the horse's chest behind the front legs, to the other side of the saddle.

GROOM

A person who exercises and cares for people's horses.

HAND

A unit for measuring a horse's height equal to 4 inches (10.16 cm).

MARTINGALE

A piece of tack that connects to a horse's girth and reins, keeping the horse from tossing its head.

STAMINA

A horse's ability to do work without tiring.

STEWARD

A volunteer who helps the judges and keeps things organized at an event.

TROT

A speed in between the walk and canter where the horse moves diagonal legs, such as the front right and back left, together.

VERTICAL

A show jumping fence made of poles or planks placed above each other.

ONLINE RESOURCES

To learn more about eventing, visit **abdobooklinks.com**. These links are routinely monitored and updated to provide the most current information available.

MORE INFORMATION

BOOKS

Aswell, Sarah. *Show Jumping*. Minneapolis, MN: Abdo Publishing, 2018.

Harris, Susan E. *The United States Pony Club Manual of Horsemanship: Basics for Beginners/D Level*. Hoboken, NJ: Wiley, 2012.

Sanderson, Whitney. *Dressage*. Minneapolis, MN: Abdo Publishing, 2018.

INDEX

ABOUT THE AUTHOR

Whitney Sanderson grew up riding horses as a member of a 4-H club and competing in local jumping and dressage shows. She has written several books in the Horse Diaries chapter book series. She is also the author of *Horse Rescue: Treasure*, which is based on her time volunteering at an equine rescue farm. She lives in Massachusetts.